front cover, original artwork by emma stace darling.
the sin of the siren by emma stace darling

emma stace ©2015
www.emmastacedarling.com

ISBN 978-1-326-35765-8

emma stace darling

the sin of the siren

For M.

protection for a blessed child

melt the sugar in a pan
add the water as you can
never stop the action, never
hanging in this gig forever
add some salt for your protection
don't you miss that sweetest section
rosemary for remembrance
mirror it for semblance
doubles everything you add
and helps forget the deal you've had
rose for all the beauty gone
violets for which you long
put them in and stir it slow
watch the seasons come and go
pepper it with corns in pink
watch it thicken, rise, then sink
add some tears for honesty
drops of blood to set you free
let it set on one greased sheet
hear the lamb of God, its bleat
once, twice, thrice, release a cry
then crush it to bits, until it's dry
watch it turning into ash
sing a prayer loud as you bash
pour the ash into a chalice
stash it in your secret palace
then set fire to it inside
and drink the flames,
you blessed child.

where we go

i shall go where i am led
you'll find me in a church

i'll find you in a cafe bar
reading the paper while you're on the phone

and i'll be praying for better times
for all the love for all the gifts
for little smiles that mean so much
for new-born babes that are not mine
for humour, yes, in all its armour
for people who need people too
for seeing things quite as they are
and not distorted thru the rain
and we go round the ring again
girls that work in bars at night
flogging myself for the sake of my plight
my own disbanded family
dad's gestures that bring joy to me

and you'll be buying frames online
eating brioche with a serviette
maybe outside, if it's sunny still
messenger slide for a cigarette

and Jesus died because he loved
i'm wondering if i will too...
not because i think i'm him
but just because i see things thru

black cat

he cleans for me
he does it all
i make a mess
he lets it fall
to show me
that i'm worth the time
those slender hands in grime.

his hands are ivory
all beauty
mine are my life
my work, my duty
but he wants
to savour
time
and prove to me,
it can be fine
to get into a weird state
be at one with all my moods
he's finely tuned to
everything i'm soaking up
and sometimes it is terror's hiccup
sometimes it's a peachy dream...
the panther moves
and oozes cream

the way he moves
and why he does it
showing off
he's mine,
and loves it

i had waited for
so long, that
i link love
with a big black cat

progress

you don't 'get me', i don't care
that need in me? no longer there.
regained my hard fought self- esteem
i zipped my zest right up its seam.
it's very comforting with work
to know, at some point, when some berk
it taking you to task in words,
ideas tweet round them, fly on, birds!
so smile and nod, and then you'll laugh
when you're at home and in the bath.
"you're missing out, big time, on stuff"
you're thinking, now it's off the cuff.
you know that you are quite, quite sane,
but have a gift, they're not the same.
unleash once more, and squat quite mad
then leap back to the lily pad
that reigns inside your head and knows
how to act normal, daily shows
some in your face head-on behaviour
artists drip a geenish flavour
you're the one that's selling thoughts
getting cheques and adding noughts
you're confident, so they find fault.
your output is your bread, your salt
you say i am 'so intense'
"i'm paid to be me. no offence".

moment

today as i was driving,
some guy let me go by
he smiled at me, and my instinctive knee jerk was to fly.
i had to stop,
'cause strauss was on bleedin' the radio
and all the rapture, dying high joy
seared right thru that place i know

vibrations, signs, humanity moving
again, and pushed out very wide
and feeling a part of a greater community
up sprang yellows from inside

that little thing, that nod of his,
it filled my tank full up with hope
and i drove on up to the corner shop
for eggs, bread, custard creams and soap.

songwriter

a songwriter was in despair
his music refused everywhere
and then he wrote shit
and he had a big hit
and now he's a millionaire

not to care

looking down, too long the sad bit
stroke my upper lip, a habit
i have seen my mother do it
burn the rock cakes, too, a bit

but when we find our parents feet
are made of clay as well as ours
innocence is lost forever,
won't come back to calm us. never.

"pip squeak daughter, you're so flirty
like your mum when she was 30"
i don't know why she gave you away
and ruined that beery summer day
in 1973.

i think a lot, don't know when to stop
watch the box and bathe in space
and change my settings, inside out
from thought, to rest, to do without
to laugh and cry and not to care
to wake and then to sleep.

to laugh and cry and not to care
to wake and then to sleep.

a mug

earthling far, far too fragile
to be left alone
or brush my hair or clean my teeth
do normal kids-can-do 'getting up' things.

i get up
fall straight down,
bruises again
the room spins
push thru it and i rise
but it's so much effort,
and i am so tired.
and there he is
holding me fast.
lest i hurt myself
again.

oh cursed me, too sensitized.
unwanted gifts
dangling carrots
tuned much too finely
a lion's mane on my wrung out shrunk head,
just to split easy, so watch it deplete me
i wish that i were the girl next door
with two point four
and a four by four
but wanting more...
i want so much less

we don't get to choose, though, do we?
fellow within-mates,
we don't get a say in it,
grates right thru me

and there he is putting me back into bed
where i've spent too much time
in my short life, this space of mine,
Christ, too much, i know, i know
he strokes my hair
and then tells me i'm
lovable
just as i am.

but it's just lies
to stop the explaining
they think i don't know
'cause i'm not complaining
they know that i'm useless
and worthless and lame

...wait till he goes to the bathroom for me,
to get some creme,
creme smelling of roses,
mum brought me from sicily?
chelsea gardens or sainsbury
i don't know where
i can't think clearly

reach into his bed-side table

but he runs back
"i'll hold you tight till you
want to live on
for the colours you paint,
the songs that you sing,
the pleasure you give us..."
"what about mine?"

"forget the big stuff
your job today's
to relax, and cuddle me,
watch rubbish tv,
and drink your endless
cups of pg"

he gets up to make it
he rushes back once more
my mouth is already full
bi-coloured tablets,
and reaching out for water
the failure daughter
i hate myself
my guilt is
quite overwhelming

he looks at me closely,
compassionately,
"you're doing so well,
you're in recovery"

but all i want is
a mug that says
MUMMY

ants

we've just been infested by ants
(i'll spare you the one about pants)
we can't find the source
thought we've both become morse
they're cheeky though, messing with giants...

who lives

during the rusty blade and her slashes
and flutter-by lashes
sit moments in life.
that horrific big thrill dipper
enforced bungee jump of woe
push out of mummy,
her warm feeding womb...

who lives?
do you?

you, who have millions
chanel in your closet
a jag outside
accessory pets?
having affairs
with people in pieces
who're possibly prettier
far more clever
than your loyal husband, he
who is keeping you
in manner of one
who lives
like a princess.
you're dead inside.

and you are drinking
more now, and more
your looks won't last
breast cancer's coming
(it's three o'clock)
and so is your gardener
who lives

with his problem
gambling debts and
his darts, then his footie
community spirit
and impish young wife,
his mates and his daughter's plight

who lives

with down's sydrome
smiling and then she cries
when she suffers from earrache
and endures her periods...

who lives

while daddy's digging

who lives

on low wages
who's tired at the end of his day
then makes love for his life
to his wife

who lives

as if it were her last day
on this earth.
lost mum and dad in a massive house fire
she was eleven.

who lives

still believing in heaven.
and smiling down at her man after loving
she silently prays
it goes something like this:

"oh jesus,
alive in me
thank you for giving me
a life full, worth living
i cherish it, cherish it
truly i do
and everything you give
to my family daily"

she kisses her husband,
and sets her alarm

when you know, you know

then storms unravelled a tied up secret
slashed wet skin, and it all sunk in
just a fact that sounded when found
you can't reject what's shot within

cord

do you feel it when i cry?
i can hear you when you sigh
a thousand miles won't cut the cord.
recall that line when i'm abroad.

scarlet ribbon

i only wanted scarlet ribbon for my hair
the spirits aware of my urgent longing
it only went for pennies
but more pennies than i had
i knew if i trusted hard enough
it would be there, come my birthday...
i just knew, the way only a child knows

i brushed out my tresses
i spent hours a day
making flaxen gold out of coarse, thick lines
when i danced and spun round around
it sprang into corkscrew curls
and the weave turned into war
as i started work again
a hundred brushes, mummy said

and when i danced and flew thru space
i felt it closer, and closer still
with every pace and jump and fouetté
i was nearer to Him
and felt so right
and felt myself deeper than i have ever felt since

i had no conscious thought
of how i looked, i did not care
about praise or approval
i only danced to get that feeling
nearer to God in my every move
leaping into His arms all day
i would die with delight
yes! at seven years old

i only wanted it for
its own beauty
i gave no thought to my own ugliness
but the red ribbon
i had seen in an old movie
moved me closer
each day and more

and so it came the special day
and the faces were expectant
it looked like ribbon
my dreams coming true

and there it was...
in blue.

there's a hole

there's a hole in my aura, dear psychic, dear psychic
there's a hole in my aura, dear psychic
a hole

then mend it, dear katie, that hole in your aura
then mend it, dear katie
then mend it
quick sticks!

with what shall i mend it, dear psychic, dear psychic
with what shall i mend it, dear psychic
this hole?

put yourself in a circle,
a ring laid
with kindling
and send everyone that you know far away

and then put all your thoughts and your love in it, also
and hide all your favourite things deep inside

and then set blue fire to it, katie, dear katie
and then throw a lit match,
stand back, watch it burn...

and dance in your circle of fire, my darling
then dance in the circle of fire
and smile

for then only the ones who adore you can enter
they'll walk thru the fire
for you and for God

and then nobody else they can enter, can enter
and you will be safe
and protected
with light

(this song is for real, for real, for real
it's pitiful, i know, you can't make it up...)

your selection

smoothing blues and burning amber for the skills you tumble forth
embracing reds and oranges and keeping very still
and little greens and violets will always head you way up north
my vision worships where you stood so long below my window sill

and terracotta cold slab tiles can make me wonder why
you chose me out of everyone, to nurture and adore
and primrose yellows, buttercups and soft the breezes sigh
the chaffinch on the orchard bough, what fool could ask for more?

i braided roses in my hair today, because i love their leaves
and sent some petals, wrapped in tissue, to two hundred friends
you tell me it was not too much, embarrassed tears wet on my sleeve
your selection makes me sigh, the stoned high never ends.

lost sight

she had lost sight...
wild flowers, chiffon covered field
her unleashed self, her untamed dogs
were traded for a shield

the letting rip that served her well
was chained up like a prisoner
and ill at ease she stood there, drowned
distorted, drawn and thinner

braided, wrapped in cornflower ties
she'd stopped crafting those ivy bows
to lace her hair, and daisy chains
and when she waves, all pleasure goes

she had lost sight...
of all the joy in sending out her petals
and calls that made her laugh for hours
the joy of whistling kettles

then struck dumb, she was terrified
for it had turned to illness
the cure for screaming, tearing flesh
is practising deep stillness...

and then she tore off her protection
resolute, inspired
she looked her demons in the eye
and challenged, they retired

she had lost sight...
in all her haste and
when it was restored

it came to her, stability
is mania's reward.

airport

the 'check-in girl' was on the phone
and working flat out on her own
abused by this guy
she did not bat an eye
'cause his bags went to dubai, his flight went to rome

storm at my window

the rumbling gets me going fast
spirit mind secure connection
strikes up sex and full surrender
(that felt rather like confession)

i want to dance, spin arms around
till in the moment, not the 'why'
the flashing makes me giddy, tranced
He's moving thru me, and i cry

i want to add to all the drama
let it pour down as it might!
be like trojan whores of nature
feel no fear and bring more light

if it's dark i'll burn some candles
then it starts, my secret night ride
see the door and twist the handle
sparked, excited, what's inside?

thru the window it's all blurry
grey, distorted valleys hidden
yes, she's there but she's not showing
like the years i spent bed ridden

there is no light in looking back
we might all get scooped up to heaven
i always felt relief in tempests
high, aged five, big storm in devon.

only passion such as this
is ever seen in times of sorrow
i get so wrapped up in bliss
i loved today, i'll love tomorrow

my numbers

i think i'll have good luck today
my numbers will come up
i feel i have the midas touch
i'm drinking from his cup

i'm thirsty and i need a break
i earned it and deserve it
today i have a place in heaven
i know that He's reserved it

and if he's vile to me again
i'll handle it much better.
the sighting of a pheasant
yes! because i'm a red setter.

i won't lean back against the wall
and slither sobbing to the floor
i'll burn his sovereign chain white hot
and scar his skin forever more

up and down his fatty legs
up and down his sweaty arms
curse the day i met that bully
singing loud the psalms

and we don't know who's in the church
we don't know who they are
and after that cold coffee morning
he was ripping off my bra

then saying sorry, over and over
i took pity on this fuck up
his sob stories, hid in clover.
now it's time to clear the muck up.

i know my numbers will come up
and then i will escape, be free
and if they don't, i still will go
he's there, my love, he waits for me.

the smallest thing

i went to brush my teeth and as
i tried to squeeze my new toothpaste
out chugged the most fantastic blue
not that with which i'm daily faced

the sizzling sweet spark in my heart
was welcome and it started
a hard slog, edit-laden day
with sun light pushing thru clouds parted.

chips

a flirty young thing, 'fish shop trix'
went straight into porn on account of her tits
she posed, over sexed
under-dressed, un-perplexed
the director said "perfect! except for the chips"

the day before

had all been done
so calmly
all considered.
i could cope
and now i feel
a quick release
from a length of rope

can be the only
final peace.

murderous thoughts
ugly, foul,
beauty romantic,
gorgeous lengths of fabric
smelling of green and pink and blue
clearly too tight
too tight tonight
too tight around my bursting mind
oh, and my abdomen too

i'm all caught up in short breaths now
sudden dismal drilled dire snippets
from some rank b-horror movie
starring me.
it's in my head.
i want to bash it
to detract from the
endless circles
sewing their notions to my heightened senses
behind the scenes footage
of darling out-takes

the day before is strangling me
but it's all over, yes,
within, without
oh God, forgive me!
get me out of this dark night!
bring the light
to this lamb
this sinner
who is ready now
to be slaughtered or saved.

it's your call
i gave my all.

longing

i want to push right thru the screen
i want to come to you
i want distortion, thru the squares
you'll see a head come thru
i want to reach so many people
want to touch the world
not close enough to touch myself
no wings, i was quite curled
i need to unravel out and to give you
all i have inside

no wonder when i feel all this
i get so sick, i hide.

if i were

one of those fortunates
who just don't care
i'd do my thing left quite alone
and i would never compare

myself to the others who
buy their perfection
and fake where they are
they whored for their connections

and they lied to buy
and have their whims smothered.
not blame myself
being one of the others

who care so much, and far too much
and needs approbation
crawling snail like, pitiful some
to the next loo-less station

and i knew where heaven
was found, aged eleven
i didn't know that
i'd be thwarted for caring
and watch my ill-faring
oh, spirited party girl
living alright on an island alone
i call it the 'fye-were'
my bliss, home made world

and what is so weird is
my friends say they want my life!
i'll leave your x factor
you'll leave your wife

i look on, they're bathing
in their ho-blow-dough
just leave me alone here
to work on my own show

class in pet names

oh! stop! no, no... minnie
you know that's not right.
relax your arms
you're dancing like a ballerina
a rigid opera singer
restricted and tight
for God in his garden, no, that's still not right
you know in your heart darling,
think about loving nights
let it all go!
move like your life will depend upon it
because it does!
you have been given the gift of performance
so offer it up
and be your own goddess,
be a queen or a whore in the dance
so now you're a changeling,
now you're like puck
and thank Him humbly for this pure luck
you won the lottery
your gifts, and so forth, so
embrace your body now and
love those sensual curves

take down your hair from that ghastly bun, darling,
get rid of all fakes, all false actors of fun
i want to see it all swish right back after you
witness your energy flow rushing thru you
and when you have moved on
(because in our time
we can never stop still)
don't you desire to leave your mark, minnie?
leave shadows behind you, for your tribe to see?

wait for your heart to dissolve into movement
the most special part of it's
stuck in you, minnie
the beauty of letting go, accept the dare
shun a mundane life, normality's fear
take risks, you of all, dare to fall on your arse!
that's it, dear, yes! just watch you dance!
do it with gratitude,
not for you, for them!
just give it all to them!
they want to receive it!

minnie, for mickey, bow down to the heavens!
the public is waiting for you
just to gift them,
so do it, and thank them, for seeking out truth!
the joy's in their faces, the air's on another plane
giving our sensual joy to them all
as many as possible in one life, dear
and lose not a moment
it's never too late.

the slightest resistance before it's too much
when embracing your partner
but never to touch...
the dearest reward is in taking their pain, minnie
if you stop dancing
you'll just die again

talent versus fame

there's so much talent in this world
and surely it would seem
it's more about luck
and who you fuck
so many stars
shine on, unseen

her moment

golden trails of buttercups will throng from yellow bowers
this hour had grown into her, as blossom into flowers
flora with its fellow fauna follow on in awe
as they dance across the moon from west to eastern shores

there are three heart splitting souls, all leaning on a tree
knowing what they want and long for, may or may not be
tilt back heads, and watch the show, attached to human fearing
what they think they need on earth might be not coming, even nearing

but one of these three channelled joy! life and love defined
for only she could own that moment, deaf and dumb and blind.

very human

i finally opened that letter today
and God, it was such a blessed relief!
i'd been waiting and waiting
like boats in the harbour
slow sway underneath
so static on top,
and so very needy for attention

it said what i needed it rightly to say
the joy, bedroom dancing, the phoning and whooping
heart pounding, adrenalin
flooding me, drowning.
for about... two minutes?

that is how it was for me

you might that think afterwards it became easier
the good news and all
that one feather entails
instead i chose to dwell on the letters
yet to be opened and what they might say
much later on in the twenty act play
the terror, the feed
my natural greed
my desperate need
for no letters
no judgement but,
just for a rest.

when will i rest?
oh, never, never

but when you go on holiday
they always forget to say in the brochures
(that they all call 'literature'
and that, they're not)
that you take yourself with you.
when you go on your jollies
they're jolly if you are.
if not, they're a drag
and a thing to get thru.

when a daisy
just is
a daisy
just is

regret

if you want to do it, do it.

who will you blame on your death bed, think on...
when you've not done what you felt you were sent for?
you'll say to God, will you, "she told me not to"
or "she said it was only destined for failure"
"he told me it wouldn't make near enough money"
all just excuses to save you the risk?

and safely you followed advice to the letter
considering her to be, clearly, your better
but where are they now?
and well, where are their legacies?
who is most loved of them?
who'll be remembered?
who will she cradle there
now and forever?

jill died of a broken heart years ago,
jean, married for dough but got woe upon woe,
and tom lost his dirty fat fortune in fire
(and now is in prison for being a liar)

and these are the people who have you here, dying
without having given yourself to this earth?
absurd, and a nightmare
a major disgrace
consider that, value it
for what it's worth...

your up-curled wider wings
never unfurled
blocked all the senses
to your unique world
you're driven to do it
but just don't know how.
it doesn't much matter

but just do it now.

high flying (the toffee and glue mix)

i want to make perfect toffee
i feel like a phoney, and sad
'cause dammit, i only put in half the butter
it's rock hard and brittle. and bad.

the smell was superb and sensational
the whole thing required little work
but italy sells quarter pounds of the yellow
and now i just feel like a berk

i bought myself two, so i thought i'd got
all right things in the mix
at that point i broke our new coffee machine
and i'm getting high from a glue-fix

but bendy toffee, it shall be mine!
i know it, i am sure
the smell is great in our kitchen space
(i think i want some more)

and i have no idea yet,
frustration set hard, i'm just short of crying
i so have to get on top of this toffee
and frankly this glue, 'cause i am flying...

if only i could

if only i could put into words
or sound
the feelings i have
sometimes
just once

they would crash into your understanding
they would swoop you right over
and crown you in sea shells and space lit treasures
and you would know that all your swimming
and deep breaths and goose fat
to go underwater
for such a long time
were never in vain...
no, never in vain
and that you saved a million

if i could play it out here
then my hands would barely touch
the keys on my piano
sweeping around the curves on a frown
as that sweet refrain comes round again

and find loving, some glorious chords
and depth of those soul aching harmonies
that only a lit soul can shine upon
the black notes would star
the white notes look paler
and i'd dance on the keys, yes
until you would weep
but with laughter, release,
with so much joy
all for you, all for you.

if only i could put them into a language
or motion or scent
that the world could connect with.
oh God,
i would do it
and now more than then.

just to feel less lonely
less impotent
driftwood
floating away from life.

humpty

said humpty "i'm done with it all"
and picked up his cell phone, rejected a call
"i think i am dying
it hurts" he said, crying
they said
"well it would, you just fell off a wall!"

sweet anima

come softly to our lovers bower
and lace my hair with herb or flower
move and touch my face and see
the rose beneath the ivory
your beauty overwhelms me so
i shut my eyes and yours will glow
right into my far wider space
my mind, my thoughts will, urgent, pace
and see your lips all day without
you near me, i begin to doubt
my own existence, there's just you
and you and you again and true
to all my promises i stand
i cannot rise, i cannot stand
without your loving sure embraces
closer yet and my hand races

and nothing touches me but time
with your sweet anima in mine

and now

and now fainting softly and into submission
i lie all in white and
my hair's like my wing
to balance me up there
as i am somewhere mid
a woman and a thing.

the last thing i heard
were the words
"count to one, dear"
i knew i would still be alert thru it all
and i am, i'm still here
(i only reached seven)

and now is this heaven?
i feel only glory
and no fear at all
of the end of my story
i look all around me,
a clearing of light
i look to the future
but see nothing there
i see that the past didn't really exist
i never self harmed once,
unsullied, these wrists.

i see only now
but its hazy in harsh light
i want to meet God
though, a sinner in deed
and in thought and in word
and in every which way, now
i only see angels and
hear bells and then i say

...nothing at all
nor want to make any noise.
oh we all talk way, way
and way too much.
when what matters
is silence
prayer
paradise found!
i look for things hidden
and lying around

and i'm quite alone here
i see that life's beautiful
for the first time
i can really feel human

and i can smell iris and lilies and roses
as if they were here right before me in posies
but nowhere they are
they are where i am, too.

i think i'm in bliss...
i don't want to pull thru.

banana skin

i wonder if banana skins
mind being the butt of a joke
like having 'willy' as your name
or hearing a word like 'poke'

and why are there so many there on the ground
just to make us trip?
but it's hilarious every time
to watch those poor sods slip

and crowds will laugh but cringe for them
as they skid on their heels or their kickers,
like when you walk out of the ladies room
with loo paper shoes, and your skirt in your knickers

but thinking more, i'll place a bet
the skins are totally up for it.
they have the last laugh, after all
it's us that look the twit!

the sun and the moon

her faintness is true to him, skimming the floor
and hazy in time lock, she's longing for more
her dance card is full up, his midnight is nigh
so leaving their hearts with each other, she'll die.

shades of lying

conquering strident, forward she walks, scarlet on a mission, focused and her face freak frozen, middle aged male just caught her stare, powerless to look away for a second, that magnet pull thing and who has the power? why would he stray from possessing this siren? still closer she paces and leaving just indents of heels in her train... imprints filled up with her need for this prey... she's at it again... this is her pattern... this is his hook.... in any hotel... he's rooted and booted, this lummox, this grey thing, this oaf of a man who thru marriage would spill it wherever he could, and solely thinking of his growing score board (and growing a beard) and one more red check by some female initial list... her sensuality silently wringing his neck, a man is enslaved to a sexual spark, she pushes him hard up against the wall with her kiss whispers "i get what i want, you could be anyone here, do you get it? you are my plaything... that is your sexual deal, take or leave it" ...and it goes on... with his arrogance, he had assumed it was kinky, the meeting and greeting, the dangerous games that she had her clown play out, just for amusement and revving his engine... he's fooling himself that she lied to protect herself... he's caught by her deeply at this moment here, and the idea of his stud-ship... being so limp and yet having such pride... plumping his feathers and boasting in wine bars... pomposity leads to our downfall, i think... and when she is done, in a month or so, who knows? she tells him it's over, and not to dare call her... and she really meant it... she'd got what she wanted, and now she was going... she'd told him the truth. on to get charlie and powder her nose, find out what she wants now and march toward getting it... his pride is in tatters, and self esteem shattered, and no more the secrets, deceiving his wife, he used to say each time that he'd been at the gym and left with his sweats in his pitiful bag... and jumps landing under the eight o'clock train... vindication, once again! and all this, solely, because he was vain enough to take her on as just one more conquest... she'd always been up front, but he had lied endlessly, everyone all the time, mostly himself... and just in case, she has a knife down her boot, her lipstick, her honour, stains still on his collar...

for blue

blue, blue fall into blue
your safe arms will see me thru
can't do wrong, there's beauty too
in your caresses when i'm thru

a great big hole has done me in
blown right thru me, yes by life
with its cat 'o nine tails, knife.
i'll never be a mum or wife.

blue will save me, i have faith
i know that nothing lasts forever
no good comes of being clever
ties are made so they can sever

we have power to know our worth
blue serenity never ends
we all wear you, gift our friends
joy will borrow as it lends

blue, blue fall into blue
i feel born again, and worth you
coy virginity's allure.
you're the closest thing to pure.

darren and angie

sat in a bar with the bloke she was seeing
he didn't see her though, because he was blind
shared the one dream, they were deeply in love
and they lived like their last day as they walked the line

bar pumping out with the mondays, the roses
she'd danced for her life, wet lips, wet hair
a snort on and off, at least she'd kicked the brown now
...so, happy times, saturdays, dream boy was there

gun shot. heard from her cubicle, couples
expressing their lust, desperation and loneliness
ran back to him "so, daz, what's the story?"
a male had been shot, and she said, soft "selfish bastard."
then "think of his wife and his kids", all compassion

but darrren: "don't bother, love, he was a right c**t,
he stole from his mrs., had her on the streets,
and his 10 year old daughter
to pay for his habit.
so he got the old petrol, and lit up a joint
and smoked it, set fire to his gaff, them all in it,
they finished a nonce off" ...but angie was trying

"at least now there's nobody left, it's all over..."
"her parents? (his too?) and their cousins? her sisters?
you are the tart with the heart, i love you"
and racing pulses, his kiss hurt her jaw thru

"and now you should know, it was him had my sight,
so dry your mascara, just get us a bevvie, doll
two pints, a chaser, a gin for me mam
a double for you, for your bleeding heart, angie
five vowels while you're at it.
so now there's one less of 'em"

no rhyme, in their dear lives. no reason, neither.
salford city deals head on with its mither.

there was no mascara, she'd had both eyes blacked
punters by wally street, didn't dare look back.
her lippy, and pound shop shades saved her from pity
and God, i so get you, oh angie, i do.

so she drank her shock out
and they had a lock-in
and under her jeans wept
fag burns thru her stocking

beauty's passing

if you see that beauty's passing
turn around
don't let it see or
let it know
it has your stare
attention, time,
or that you laid bare

only let that beauty pass
tell yourself
it has nothing you want
or crave or does you good, in deed
in thought, or gives out what you need

it's the crowbar separation
when love's waiting at the station
beauty passes thru...
so normal
but it harms
distracts
won't match
inside or out
with what's within
or what's without
you'll see?

when you feel that beauty's passing
say thank God
and throw your head back
smiling as you
stand beloved and
yes, stand tall, before the crowds

as you build more castles in the clouds

rainbow minus one

i cannot show you all my colours
though i'd like to, dear...
it's true i am a rainbow
only minus one is there

if i gave you all my soul
and all my heart and mind
i would give you so much pain
you'd deafen or go blind

i can give you everything
a husband ever needs
or wants or loves or just enjoys
and these are good, like seeds

they're my essence, all my love
they're the real me.
but i won't give you every shade
you'd die at what you see.

faith and the frog

the shy, greasy haired, anorexic in the corner thinks no one can see her... so the spot light's shining out from her solar plexus and reaching out to those who know... who see the other side instead... i am with the three other sisters, dressed in feathers, they know, they know, what i know, they do... we all open our sandwiches, she gets out of her pocket a calm looking frog and she licks up it's back, and sucks out the venom, and while we feel in our pockets for our phones but find instead emergency lillets and tissues and keys... this woman shoots up from low on her knees... then she starts a-spinning, to her own inner drum... first slow as a turtle then fast like a tiger, the music she heard was full, bright green harmonies and still nobody looked but we four wowed girls, holding hands tight so as not to break the circle... we trusted her and would protect another sister... faith had kissed it... and the prince and his poison pleased her so much that she just started smiling, with one gold tooth, her hair became full bodied, fresher blonder, bouncier, like chris in the white rooms, and her make up highlighted her sharp individuality, she formed highest brow arches, geometric cheekbones and a full bottom lip, which she was licking, and as she was moving we felt empathy, trancing... can you hear me, doctor...? we might need you, which doctor? no, doctor of psychiatry? no, well then, dr. who? yes. on stand-by and eating his baguette and hip flask full of who knows what, ciggies in pocket... when you think of her dancing, well, this was not that... a whirling, lustful dervish, forming frenzied curves and large heavy breasts, a tall woman, a real woman at last! a waist and hips that housed the moon, i suspect, we could hear the melody she was hearing, and though pretty cloudy it was clear enough... what we saw was heaven in a female and flying wild boar and bears that caressed her, fish that stroked her there and there... the colorado river toad holds a prize called my dement, or 5-MeO-DMY, for short, there are tryptamines within, you see, and let there be no ambiguity... what took over was real, true. as real as the three girls, who knew the gatekeepers, the keepers of the keys, their daily lament, the deeper the sadder, the sadder the more joy, they're one and the same air, to my kind of girl, yes! ...and so were we as high as her just for we are the family, the lovers of the goddess within, only supporting our venus nest building, at home there, inside our new friend and out bonding... and girls can feel so much in tune and synchronise their pretty selves with the red out-going tide... and faith, she was laughing, raucous belly laughing, vain giraffes, fearful of ageing were modelling so many silk scarves, made beautiful india look like the co-op, and penguins skateboarded and just took her hand, yes... and led her to the waters edge, and to the sand...and if we get close like this, it's God inside us, he made toads and monkeys too and all the jets of light that shine thru you... she flung out all her hand bag stuff, her oyster, handcuffs, parking tickets, passport, some lip balm, a wallet, a fountain pen (out of ink), and eye-lash glue... nobody gathered it up to protect her from thieves who prey on a life force like this... an empty vessel who's channelling something... but we were there, the sisters, the inner eyed four, and this was all for an hour or more... and she runs up and eyes are wide, pupils dilated, and saliva dripping, oh! God bless the humble, their gates of escape, their hiding and outing... oh! how can this glory not be made by God, this anecdote, this tale of faith and the frog.

rose

a big beaky drummer called rose
was blind as a bat, as it goes
the outcome of this
was a bit hit and miss
because rose used to follow her nose.

fucked up

larkin's wrong.all christians, muslims,
hindus, buddhists, war must cease
it's not your mum or dad that fuck you up,
it's our attempts at peace

hung jury

we must never judge each other
it's like setting fire to rubber
hiding your new baby's face
or faking grace, or mocking faith

while you're wrapped up in assumption
"so pathetic, where's her gumption?"
in the ether with her mother
house fire, ashes, child and lover.

thought i was the litter's runt
now i reign as queen of c**t
cheater caught, i thought i knew you,
sex will sell, but this we knew

she knew he was king of gays
and turned a blind eye, church on sundays
the entire tenor section
rosaries round his erection

when i'm confident i swear
but my respect for God is there
trail gaze squinting in my twelfth Hail Mary
saw you hanging from a cypress tree

clarke

"we're all so sorry to hear about clarke"
"well, we had no fun, it just all lost its spark
and i really resent
that he seemed quite content
so i shot him. was that a bit quick off the mark?"

i know

i could weep, and weep i do
when they say "oh, what's the use?"
don't they know that all weak minds
can deeply drown out all the truth?
water will always dissolve the blood
like a drunken, wine stained, cheap suited slut.

when a lamb bleats
we don't say "what's the use?"
we hear it sharing with another...
and then we might say to each other
"listen to that lamb cry out
i wonder what it's saying"
all who will weep
for a flock of sheep
must gently ask
"but,why?"
and never be ignored
no, never be ignored

you know when a human
needs attention
you know when it wants
to be quiet.
it will stop
and sit in silence
melting it out
all the pain that is trapped inside
oozing, spilling it all about
and then it's purged.
it's out

and maybe we
won't ever know
if that soul is
all wrung out from trying
with the never
ending crying
the wringing of hands
and endless sighing

but i catch you, smiling
and know that you're dying

worry about money

all that worry about money's
simply wanker's doom
it doesn't make it grow on trees
or stop the endless gloom

it only causes navel gazing
and it makes you dwell on lacking
as it eats away your hours that
sure won't help you, stopping, 'slacking'

my advice to everybody's
never worry about money
idiotic, mindless, futile,
neither worth head space, nor funny.

on the money-worry front
once, twice, thrice i say desist!
better yet, go down the jockey
have a laugh, get pissed.

i thank you.

dream

take me where your sail boat drifts
harbour me in a sacred place
a silent white lace, wet leaf gift
that i can nurture, and with grace

honesty

she reaches out, this woman there... to touch the track lines on his arms...
the train tracks are not more scarred for life, they could be built over by
some man, easy, facile, just dug up and concrete covered... feel him girls...
for honesty... and wonder why you never did it... for freedom you will look
to the hills, and pray there when you want ascension... was he doing it for
attention, little boy lost in his mothers heart... a leaf on the line... don't know
where i got this from... from is 'form' to dad and me... and is 'adn' but just to
me... look to the hills, stretch out and see those ants a-marching... striding
forth in waves and lines so powerful... they'll get trojan whores if necessary,
one step ahead and ideas pouring... sweet is the enemy in life's kitchen...
fruit not biscuits need our mouths... it's how you choose your temple's
food... we will be careful how we use our sweetness... feel it girls, for we
are tight... even sisters, a million steps... seven million, forty million, eighty
billion breasts, and women holding hands... feel those marks, trace them
yes, but we're not scarred yet... so raw and painful... more to her eye than
the monkey guy... not as wincing as the searing agony of looking right
behind his eyes... all dark and vacant... take note of those ants... magnify to
see they're strength... and then we kill then just because they're there... much
like the girls from every corner of the globe... circumcision, Christ above, i
bleed for these girls, how can i stop it alone? free flow fear, anxiety's slaves
because we're scared to worship our goddesses overtly, out there, burnt for
all to see... we're cruel jailers, track marks on the footpaths legal or illegal...
who makes those laws? i piss in their fields and the grass just thanks me... a
shower of gold, bending bowers... don't own land but claim it, virgins and
prostitutes alike... unite! and fair exchange... men have it easy, uni tasking...
jobs and respect, given without asking... feel the damage of fifty thousand
years... our sensuality's punished, you see... they're slapped on their broad
long backs, we're sluts, that same act, the very same giving and taking... eye
to eye she hits the floor... just love and a bouquet of honesty... oh! yes! and
she'll never want for more... floating want and hidden desire in case she's
done for arson right there... there, there and even there... ooh, so good and
sent from heaven... the number that comes to me is seven... sisters, yes...
and there's the link... so look towards the sky and fly... you're gorgeous in
your element... sober or flying an elephant, child... and words are coming,
words are lightning, flashing thru her little frame... men can often feel the
same but won't get whips and lashes so, though she does solely for painting
her lashes... oh, the radiance of owning yourself... it comes and goes like the
postman, dear... curiouser and curiouser as he comes near... what will he
bring, a letter from him...? anything owns you... an empty envelope will fill
her her up till the end of time... it's wasted time which wilful stands the

greatest crime... self pity... we're all enslaved to one thing or other... impossible as getting love form your brother, or seeing your mother suffer on, being impotent to stop it, that's a man's song that sings and sings out and silent each time, no rhyme... illness comes at any time... it's all in the mind... it's all in time... then thinking fast in scan and rhyme and reaching out to see what a woman sees... oh, girlfriends look towards the fine designs... then walk past when it doesn't don't feel true... when we know our minds we're all forces of nature, we're shudderingly powerful when we know... and what we do... this one's for you... my friend, my love, my sweet guru... well, you are one of those, you too, following suit, it's wonderful... and sometimes we all want, want, want to be you, the dark days, flooding sleeves and wet dripping from our noses, yo-heave-ho, connection like this only comes in posies... floral tributes from the Lord... it isn't a woman, made by any earthling... this is from above, high up and all around us, sometimes we see it... sometimes we don't want to be a man... though they want us to... women chairpersons, boyish figures, clothes horses, coat hanger shoulders, and anorexia rules our world... well, you keep on trying and make a man out of me but you fuck us up, our breasts are used by him for self pleasure fodder, magic ladies, computers machines, they'd rather watch others connect than do it themselves, no risks, safety, a porn star won't hurt you she'll always tell you that you're king kong... the best, the biggest of them all... but you're an ant, we all are really, watch the hills, they move me, barmy... delicious girls, breathe it in... walking thru the valley deep, and hiking on, still wide asleep... and loving the wild flowers, hearing their incantations, smiling, and i'll go with them for today... i'll stay with safety, and we are women, even if they cut out our wombs, sew our sex up, lop off our breasts... no pain, just wiser and look to the sky, girls, here we go, the rabbits flying again... a million white balls of fluff are a-hopping, right above our heads, right now... and if you give in, then, you're dead, you see, if you quit, you're dead... his purple, red blue veins all lumpy and gristly and sticky, and stinking too, infections that will have his arm off... i can't tidy, he has to throw out junk... but he thinks of it as defining his spunk... he needs it 'ok' now... says God was cruel to him... and it was costly... but i think that God is that bouquet of honesty...

the fine line

i walk along the finest line
illusion and reality
but every time it always ends
in infinite finality.

artists

artists don't ever need money
for rent, bills or filling their tummy
they should work for free
still, we buy them drinks nigthly
they're using us! i'm using irony

that saw

there was no jig about this saw
pushed forth and backwards deep in my skull
and jammed and bent to harm me more
a crucifixion? not enough pain

there was no wincing, no clenching movement
i sat still, said prayers to endure it, but then
in barbarity's pride, only one stride sent
not putting me out of my misery

when you first burnt me, you cut that steak
that saw is what your eyes became.
physical agony's just a dull ache
compared to the sear of the lover's rejection

security check

i stand at the gates and wait to go thru
i dare not look back
but i know you're there
waiting to see if i've gone away, safe
it's never quite safe
when they take me from you.

i cannot say good bye, no, not ever
i can't just invite in the sorrow it brings
how can i leave you when i am not there yet
oh, how can i leave you at all?

yes, i am safe at security check
they checked my safety, and found it was lacking...
so He took me thru to His gates up there
for once and for all
and held me so fast
in His loving arms
on the other side

Jesus was held on the other side, too
he brought others joy, but he felt only agony
good bits, i'll give you, but one life of pain
but then he was safe with His Father again

safe in sardinia
with those who love me for
who i am,
not what i do

my father loves me for who i am
i felt him there
i feel him here
as i embrace
others
i also hold dear

check my security
sometimes i bleep

pressure to engage

i must engage in life once more
get up
wash hair
get dressed
leave bed
this wretched couch, damned safest haven
where sole mental torture grabs me
and it does, its does, it does.

brush my my teeth oh! not again!
it's so exhausting
i could sleep for a week right after
but never do, just fitfully
and dream i'm eating my own faeces
or being gang raped all over again
or re-live that lame overdose
when i was not as i am now

they're all right off my christmas card
list, and i couldn't write them
it's been thirty years now,
i'll try again and...
i can't finish things, you see
full of self loathing
i'm back to my bed
and treated like barrett
the queen wimp of wimpole street
when i'm so sure
i could rule the world
oh i could do it if i were just well.
i'm just shot to pieces, you see?

engaging in life
red pressure runs rife
it's every reflection
i see in my knife

"i should, i should, i should, i should"
i'm shoulding all over myself, again
and feel such guilt, as they clean up my mess
lament my past and dread my fate
ashamed to my breast, and further still
as i watch others 'doing', when
i can't do 'being'
without fear of falling,
and faint with fatigue
thought myself to a coma
and comatose, wide awake

oh Lord, have Mercy,
and just let me sleep

leaves

i ask myself if leaves have feelings,
and i think they do
like dogs and trees, the moon the breeze
yet i stand unconvinced by you

the power of the written word

to say "i love you"
it's written forever.
put in your lace box
and thrown away never.

or to note
"semi skimmed and bread"
just to be able not to forget.

to read
"five thousand pounds only"
with your name, mid stave

or
"i've left you, and taken the kids"
with a post-it stuck on your microwave

petal

i picked a petal
from a whole bouquet
of dozens, father, would be lovers,
roses, pinks, the scents had flushed me
this one was brown
so i kissed it away

no need to say i chose the
flower most lovely for my boy
so separate from all its sisters
by his side of the bed, for joy

thought i'd given the queen of them all
for giving's sake. instead...
that perfect stem in a tall green glass,
within hours was dying, nearly dead

abel

there once was a horsey called abel
who liked to be tied up with cable
and boogie at nights
with his flash fairy lights
but they all labelled abel 'unstable'

well, my trusty shrink thinks
that this judgment stinks,
this horse is magnificent!
abel's just 'different'

yes, i won't go there

i'm running down the aisle of a church somewhere in spain... don't know where... never been there... and they were there for a huge celebration, then the reception and three tiered floral confection, but not for me, not the white for me, not for this girl, wearing red... what happened? was i doing my distorted thinking, did i go off on a cloud again? you take them on, a dirty girl, or was it real, a hardened man, all bearded which i loathed in him... a fine looking hurt and bitter man whose heart turned to stone and this child i saw, he had no chin, i liked the package... i thoroughly enjoy being so very shallow yet so deep, 'sad is happy for deep people'... you can't wed someone you don't know at all... or maybe it's better... how would one know? it's so hot and the scent of fresh oranges mixed with the incense makes me turn and walk away... i want to marry Jesus, not some hunky teenage dream... the lust i have for anything churchy, the icons tell me to take a closer look, and Mary says "girl, take it in, you just don't love him, it's the dream you love", over powering, the insight and clarity... it was a hook! it was a hook but i didn't know to go with it or not... all change... bring the boats in... the planes, trains and taxis too... i chose to gather my long crimson skirts and reveal my manolo's and my stocking tops, and fast i rode away with my train, far away from my dream and not knowing, not knowing it, all based in wine and too little stimulation too little reading, museums and working too hard, time to make up stories that should be written and not lived out, or lived thru or tried to be made real, the worst... that goddess perfection being my retreat and my interior world, smaller by the hour by then... and they were all looking at me not incredulous, but accusingly... so i picked up my speed, God have mercy! i turned my heel in the grating, i fell over hard, and crashed down on the marbled floor, and broke my ankle and right arm too, and worse still, i had ripped up my new dress, and half way down (not up) the longest aisle, i saw him approaching all suited and muted, and froze like a smack addict looks at a kilo... and there he was, right there and standing before me, oh, where is oramorph right when you need it? i checked, but no pockets or hand bag or wallet... where is the antidote, calm i achieved in the spring time in england of 2/'14? the start of my wellness, wilful self control... don't catch my eye... don't look at me... you are becoming a ghost to me now... who never replied when you should have been swimming from your door to mine to my aid in the hospital... you were with your friend who'd had his foot cut off, oh, the irony! well now i'd messed up limbs, and you are still there, caring with three feet and annoyingly fine... this shouldn't have happened! it should never have gone this far, it was a dare i pulled off with satan, in whom i don't even believe, i misused my powers to make him a fall, falling tower, tiefer und tiefer, felt such a high, but then came the low and desperate and sad... looking at me on the ground he was... two people stuck, removed from surroundings, in little boxes neatly painted... i struggled to get up and with all my might and force i dragged myself passed him, each lurch agony, lost a shoe- the horror of thwarting my life time's passion- i brushed past him, the only touch we were ever to have, just keep on, keep heading for your safety zone... it shouldn't have gone this far, don't look back, don't look back... keep going, and never look back... you know it's the right thing... the worst exit ever... i looked back, eurydice! well girlfriends, he wasn't looking at me, but was on his cell phone... and, on his side of the church... one limp girl, one of the female admirers appeared in a white dress and walked down with daddy, the man from my nightmares was back at the front... i stood crucified all bent over and hopping, armless and harmless, don't pity me, pity please, just don't do it... watching the opening solemn doors and flood in the mighty light, sick, the sunlight and chose to watch it unravel... the incense made me so faint and the vows... i heard Mary cry to me "go home and love him and hold on so tightly, hold fast, hold fast and you won't dream it again" ...then he turned to walk back down the aisle with her, thinner puffed up hair, darker than me, and too much make up and ballet pumps. my God! i thought, is that really what he wanted? ...she was adoring her new husband, giggly, and he looked, well, just sort of sorted to me... she looked so low maintenance, she caught my eye and i was surprised, for i really smiled... true joy for them, joy, untold content, freedom from my misplaced illness and self-harm addiction... now i won't ever crawl again for a fix, and looking at my phone will not make it ring... the glory of right thinking... and when i forget, i will ask Holy Mary... for she always knows, like my mum always knows... i never wanted to go to spain, and hardly surprising, i won't go again. i forget the rest. yes, i won't go there again.

when it goes

round n round 'n' round they go
like tape around her radio
trying to sidle and slide round the blast
like trying to keep a lost love from the past

endless circles, words just flying
meaning all melted, like lard when it's frying
you cannot hold her fast in your glance
you knew when you felled that last one tree of chance

sticky tape loses its sticky in time
but you can't say one stick in time'll save nine
for she's still a-twirling around like a baton
your love life's silk tie has still got some fat on

so bye bye two, and hello you
blood red changes into blue
future? better or worse, who knows?
and who knows where love goes,
when it goes?

ice pack

the sear of your eyes

i'm stippled with goose bumps
i was sure but
now i'm just sore.
ravaged by nettles
that you just ignore.

you can't help but feel it,
i know you, so see how
i'm known now in braille
my body reads
"just give me warmth
you're in here,
please stop trying
to paint me and fail."
there's desperation wet in the trail
bloke on a tractor
drives over a can
there's muck on your conscience
and mud on the van
"please stop trying to make me a man."

as you drive off, of course,
you don't look back
i am a lit match here
and you are an ice pack.

just wandering

walking thru the streets
of red arched bologna
what does she see from under her hat...

students lounging and chatting away
eating single pizza slices
rolling tobacco
it's cheaper that way
laughing, loving, kisses, romance
dreadlocks and spikes
and books in a mess
sometimes reading
with a can in their hand
silver jewellery and beaded stuff
the uniform tattoos
forever, they think

pace, pace, pace rhythm
it's for my health, you see

further on, two minutes ahead
women waft in furs and coats
hermes handbags perfume float
and cardboard rope-held shopping bags
either alone, yes, alone in the most part
or with little dogs on long leashes for freedom
oh, the bitter irony!
thinking of time lost, or wasted or squandered
think of their doctors, their mothers, their daughters
i hear their thoughts out loud sometimes
and it mostly makes me sad for them
sometimes though, it's bearable

pace, pace, pace rhythm
it's for my health, you see

i see men in bars or stood outside them
drinking a coffee, a tiny espresso
or having corretto to spirit themselves up
thinking their thoughts
one step at a time
practical clothes and practical chat
they talk to each other about all their workload
their cars, and their taxes, their crudo suppliers
brotherly talk, in a slowed down way
and sometimes they stand there alone and complete
it's easy to watch them at peace with themselves

the arches
the arches
they steal your attention
we are those arches
yes, in our own way

pace, pace, pace, rhythm
it's for my health, you see

find your way home, girl
get comfort in somehow
enough of this walking
it's been hours now
the mouse is still silent
the lion still roars

you just saw a snippet of life.
it was yours

all change

solitude has been
my only constant
my sole companion
got on pretty well
allowed for each other
and i felt looked after
and knew where i was
in the depths of despair,
in joy, or in prayer
i knew i was there.

today it will all rearrange
like a puzzle
and might be a muddle
a mess of my 'haves'
and those things that i had
but looked over or hated
but knew them so well

i will move back into
my home today
and back into
you

but that's not what they say

me fever

i must go down to the sea again
prosaic, i'll tell you for why
i left in the sand a set of silk undies
a pervert could nick 'em, i'd die!

that girl

oh you would give your everything
just to be that girl.
she's always the same, she's always on form
her social life's a whirl.

she never has anxiety,
she pays for drinks each time
she's gentle hearted, confident
her breasts are pert, her skin is fine.

and she is normal, she's just super
and she's found her guy
she jogs around loving life in the city
greeting people, chin worn high

and she is kind and grounded too
she loves the things one has to do
this girl's life just flows so easy
she doesn't seem to struggle thru

when we go out, she's pink all night
she never fades to blue
oh how you want to be that girl.

(but that girl only wants to be you).

in laughing

i'm finding myself more in laughing
not singing
or writing
or painting
or posing

my jaw less gripped
my neck relaxed
for once i don't care
if i'm perfect or crap

i find myself in laughing.
i intend to do it more.

christmas window

there was a child outside a store
at Christmas time, all twinkling, colour
reds and greens and golds and more
i needed to connect with her

she seemed in some strange state of grace
more charm than everything shiny inside
all rosy on a porcelain face
quite transfixed, her eyes held wide

what was this darling longing for?
there was a tree, a bear, a lolly
soldiers, santa, drums, yet more
the joy! although she wasn't jolly

she seemed so soulful for a kid
she was alone, aged six or seven
i wondered what she normally did
where were her folks? in the shop, or in heaven?

i asked myself if she were real
a shaft of light shot from her eyes
and gazing thru the pane's tight seal
she was all lit, like festive fires

but i crept forward pace by pace
her coat was red, and never worn
this child was wearing tights of lace
otherworldly, and forlorn

amaze! this glow, this luminescence
was it only i who saw?
was i in an angels presence...
(who could ever ask for more?)

and she was talking to the shop doll
she was hearing answers back
then she laughed and seemed to loll
and then without the glass's crack

she was the doll in the window's show!
frozen, same pose as outside.

what i'd witnessed, i don't know.
but magic comes at Christmas tide.

deadline

the urge is to get ever nearer, closer
to see what is under the sea's other side
to touch its air, to fill up my senses
stretch out my own fins, hold them open wide

i want to dance upon the edge
not tethered up in an open space
i need to feel what they must feel
while scales scratch over my skinless face

i wonder, would they swim off somewhere forever
would i be considered their foe?
my guess is that if i dared cross that fine line
they might as well tag my toe

when your sisters sing

softly swinging on my love
-the branch of giving- sits the dove
the cooing calming neutral presence
soul ease, cool relieving essence
you can perch on me all day,
all night and still in slick star bright
when the day comes, you'll be there
and i'll support you, naked, bare
in winter, autumn russets, spring
and summer, when your sisters sing
to look around oneself is bold
but i don't do as i am told
i just act as i feel i should
feathers don't say
"i was good"

enigman

where are you now, my peter pan boy?
when i need you, you are there
when i don't, you're found nowhere
i can sense you, then you fly
but i know that you're there

this is no epic of drama and lust
you are the anima inside my own
heart and head and body and all
your lithe back bone stretched out forever
like a fish or an alligator,
your side is your throne

you are perfection and i fall so short
you are too beautiful, my mind's mill
is caught, stuck in stillness, as you're gliding thru
i gave you my life, boy, so do as you will.

you say you're an alien
maybe you are
that would explain your behaviour
i'm sure.

enigma,
my enigman,
don't go, 'cause i'm yours

on a letter

took years on a letter
one
just one.
writing
rewriting
adding
typing
rubbing it out
and screwing it up

it grew into beauty,
streaming perfection
just
what i had wanted to say.

(a whole year of tears
in a paper cup
she'd drank from
all that time ago
i filled it once
i filled it twice
and washed with it,
a salty price).

and i never sent it
because i so meant it

yellow praise

yellow dilly
yellow dilly
so beautiful in your heavy head and strident body
trumpet all your glory out
herald spring time in

in my head i feel gladdened duty
yes, it's you who bring good news
always welcome (always perfect)
i'll make scones and jam for tea
and waft outside, admiring you
in all your golden worship worthy

but...
i'll leave you there
as i come in
bare footed, wet and
marks on my floor.

dew, dew
lovely you
i have my own secret too

tell me lady daffodil
are you joyful when we hold you in our hearts?

with your great importance, yes!
the burden of that certainty
that times are changing
nothing can stop it
only you can bring the news

and have we caused our final measure
gathering you all up for our pleasure?
for some joy inside our shell?
are we making bad moves well?
when you bud, it's in the air
when you blossom,
God is here!

daffodil you duly do me
with your serendipity
laden with the purest charm
of future seasons coming-in.
daffodil you do me in
just with your natural sap and skin

oh! daffodil you win!

living alone is a wonderful thing

she felt the call, the drum beat of 'now' and so she went down... winding winding... curling stairs, serpent tail steps... carrots in hand, as there were every time... and after she was spiked in the bare foot twice by a nail and a flint of stone, she felt no more pain... as the growing intensity of the rosa mystica incense lifted her high up beyond the fourth floor and more... she looked thru the trunk... left open for invocation... of course not to dare lay her hands on the treasure, an era of old love letters, usual stuff... but to find her wand, place her right hand around its shaft... her grandfather's wand... and she struck her arm out and made herself warm with that familiar fizz of the call for making magic... a little girl there in the body of a woman... she breathed in the perfume, the dust and the past... and she made it last till her first set of layers were lost... Jesus lost all his layers but in a much worse way, but his mum was Mary too, he was all spirit... she was simply taken... taken over... as she opened up the old gramophone... and put on a 78 of tribal sounds... and began to move just very gently... she closed her eyes... she let her long grey hair down from its bun with two pins which she put in her pocket with her pills... and smiled and was young again... putting on his cloak, putting on a stranger... the one he had worn lined in brightest red satin, all inky outside and not a speck of dirt on it... she sat in a whirl of his cloak... wand in hand... in between her toes she squeezed agate, aquamarine, garnet, cornelian, jet, amber, jade and peridot, and put his gold rings on her left hand... she put his top hat on, then took it off again and out jumped the rabbit she'd always called 'truth'... running about the room, fed it the carrots... and then she scratched her arm up, right up her sleeve... and out came whole bouquets of just picked fresh flowers, not silken, one, two, three, four, enough to scent the entire room... she sat very still and she sealed her eyes with essence of dewdrops she had in a canister... as the music surged she found herself rocking... who knows for how long, as long as it took... and there she was taken... her eyes opened slightly, her eye balls were now raised to the heavens... there she repeated the words that free fell to her open, unfolding dear lily of a mind... an old enchantment... some spell or other... she offered it to God and then she felt safe... as when she was in her grandaddy's arms, in front of the fire, eating toasted food on his long thin fork that he put in the flames... in which she saw fairies... not picture book ones... the real ones that come forth to those who have eyes for them... he used to play music from the movies, good night sweetheart and its sisters, but what she could hear, as she lay there all curled up against his chest, was this sweet incantation, the same beat that she was listening to now... in a white way she was back in the womb, men have no wombs so it can't have been that... and now she is in the place, now she can feel it all, now she can be what she always wanted to be... free from all burdens, all discomfort, notions of what we must be to be normal and healthy... she was all spirit and it had consumed her and finally now she could go in peace... as she never wanted to leave that room... and she never did... during one of these trances, her ritual dances... when she came to it was three weeks later... and twenty years younger, each time, once again... she packed it all away and went upstairs hungry to watch something crap on telly and eat alone happily, with such an appetite. living alone is a wonderful thing.

etta

i worked with an actress called etta
so foul, no-one dared to upset her
selfish and rude
always in a bad mood
so i spat in her drink every night to feel better

whoopie-do!

whoopie-do! i love you
it's reciprocated too!

on the bus their phones all ringing
i just wanna burst out singing!

it's all scanning now and rhyming
you appeared, amazing timing!

twin souls meet, a new day dawning
(blimey, talk about no warning!)

they're all moaning, tired, yawning
in my heart, on a big huge awning
your name, my name, in the sun
'cause one and one makes... one!

whoopie-do!
dreams comes true
God smiled down
on me and you
so... everything is want to say is
whoopie do!
and thank you.

pre-med realization

i was caught up, in the webbing of time
a stem rose drop traces straight down the long lime
there's something horrific and also ecstatic
in knowing that now, it can never be mine.

ripe the blood

when the house was far away
and doctors ran to tend to her
the boiled water, tendered cool
was dabbed on skin, on sick and drool

when the kitchen had some mice
and the cooks had rage for them
she was green and fevered still
the priest ran o'er the hill

her brother flew with a horse and knife
his head crashed down praying at her side
and she did open evil eyes
and tell him of her wicked lies

and of her many lovers, games
and dragged him thru the orgy's play
but he who loved this cold, cold heart
would never leave when she depart

and never feel the cooks raw rage
in his possession, his obsession
he'd hidden forbidden their lust together
he would shroud it sweet, forever
still he'd love her beyond the grave
and pine for his sister, hurting, brave.

when you went

just for a couple of weeks...
we kissed, we talked
we knew it was nothing
just some time apart.
i work here
you work there.
a fact of love
a practical matter.

but as the mornings came and came
i changed inside then outside too.
slower, more deliberate
colours muted
sounds all deepened
and the light dimmed
slower than slow
then hunger went
and make-up, too
ready to say "i'm coming" to you
never, no, never,
please, don't leave me
i know that i could ne...

i sat on my bed
and tilted my head
and softly you said
i had the look
in that moment there
of a young deneuve.
vintage film atmosphere.
sorrow all around me
black doves sympathising,
so, pity all poor lovers, do.

i dared not play music
for it would so touch me
and move me too deeply
that i might die.
and yet, your kisses
moved me more than my ravel

yes and yes
for my ascension

black black black black
that 'oh no' black,
in those deadliest of mornings
entrancing, slow, and strange, intriguing
do i really know you at all
mister deep and deeper waters still ?
i've gone deaf
but i still hear you call.

i heard the car door shut.
and didn't look out
well, one tiny time
my snatched window-crime

saw the champagne of your rotary watch
(i'd bought and gifted you)
gleam thru the bushes
on your adonis wrist
and then i saw you taken away...
in a haze of
cut-glass,
a sunlight's squint
and knew all hell ensued from then.
i work here
you work there.
a fact of love
a practical matter

and though i grow in solitude
and i fare well, alone
i feel you inside me,
souls rising...

and i am safe again.

swings

when i burst forth into wit and jokes,
and out of control laughter
i feel it tighten in my soul,
for fear of what comes after

walking talking

love great tufts of absinthe dirt!
cows don't ever look 'alert'
and sheep have square eyes, so i'm told
pigs are clean, until they're sold

i make animal noises loud and bold
and i don't care if i'm "too old"
stallions swish off flies, God like power
and goats are great (till they give you that glower)

but oh, to shout 'ave maria' aloud
and call in conviction, instead of in shroud
at night in bed when you're alongside your lover
whispering's hard, and too hot under cover

to feel that prayer going straight up to heaven
the end of lent, eating sweets when you're eleven
lily will come back in less than three days
tonight i want ice cream and not bolognese

oh please make him not be there waiting uphill,
after the joy of the jam comes the pill
grant me more faith, God, that's all i will ask
then i can roll in wanton bliss on this grass

i'm walking and talking
faith's furness burned tatters
i know i need more of it
that's all that matters

runaway bride

the veins you yield are
intricate
deliberate
and a web of perfection.

none of them are ever touching
all of them cling to the spine
a tiny binding or a baby
one, you see, for the learning chart
looking at them with a child-like heart
it'll end your day before its start
you'll see likenesses and smile

this leaf, for sure, had a story to tell
if i spoke 'tree' i would listen well
details of its history
and find out how the angels perch there
eat their viennese whirls for tea
while bouncing up and down they laugh
and sip their cups of mushroom tea
gosh, i'd love to join them there
(and) you're not permitted to come with me!

looking at this leaf, oh, i see
canada, devon, and mystery
i wonder where it floated from
and how it feels when trodden on
i want to ask what sounds it likes
and if a kiss is impolite
i love it and i'll walk home holding
my gift for the groom today

i open a card, put the leaf inside
it's gone. another runaway bride

seaside rendezvous

i know i can get it
but do i really want it?
it could be salty in the sea air
it could be catching in her salty hair
she's drumming her fingers
over his shoulders
and he stinks of the tar that
you find on the beach
a seaside brothel
is not the only thing fishy here
sticky with vaseline

i know that i'm nearly there
but do i want to be here?
or it could be
squawking in the skies
dripping down on us here
like God or the big eyes
that follow us everywhere
she's rubbing her rouge
over the back of her hand
and her riffa is stuck to her
bleach scented lips

i know that it's coming
why do i draw it in so?
when i could be
pure, like the harps
from the heavenly symphony
the laugh of the child
the surprise in her face

as i take off my stockings
i'm putting on a stranger...
as i take off my stockings
i'm putting on a stranger...

something new

(to be read slowly and softly)

something new and shiny, true
poles repel, they pull us, too
but that's not all i was to you
the change that i was going thru

though i was chained, i found a soul
i dared to touch it, found a hole
a place tattooed in grass and coal
my name, my voice, my face, my role

was just to metre out your mess
i ached for it, though, i confess
to all distorted thinking, not
to woo, but neither to impress

i needed what you held inside
you always looked calm as you lied.
your yearning heart was open wide
and never thought i'd darken, hide

and you had no hooks, you were bold
you fat old drunk with nothing to hold
and tenderly i will unfold
and sing about what i've been told

something new and virgin white
so i'll tell it to the night
and gently i'll live on and fight
and what i fear most will feel right

just like me

and on my hike it caught me. glimpsed
the smallest flower i ever saw...
wondered if at her conception
she said too 'but i want more'

life

today i was in heaven, people,
dancing with an angel
today i felt the air resist
and heard the atoms, each with its bell

i moved thru all resistance
and i saw the lights upstairs
i'm glad i have been targeted,
and spinning unaware

i turned and stopped and made a shape
a grand facade, a saucy end
pastiche of being bare bucolic
carved around my burlesque friend

the first lone minute to the last
i learned to give, and i learned fast
my legs all muscles taught and straight
then bending in submissive state

i was beneath the clouds, and just,
and hair abandoned, loose and wild
and i was wearing sweats with dust
and i, so limber then, quite mild

i bent right back and touched the floor
the joy is in the dance, you see
my head was sliding, wanting more
and i came home to agony

'cause in livorno or en route's
my bracelet, gift of purest beauty
five trains, buses, cafes, loos
st. anthon please, just do your duty

it was my boy's at birth, you see
i can't believe it's not mine, now
i hope it will be loved, not sold.

i sort of feel it's in the sea

a poem a day

a poem a day keeps the doctors at bay
my joys, my fears, it does the job better
(i use the page to exorcise rage),
in fact, it does it by the letter.

i work it all out, right out, just so
stories, my diaries, sit again, bound up tight
just as i felt before thrashing it all out
choked, lump in throat, in the strangling night

first you think that you're are over the bridge
then you think, but what was that for?
just a load more hourly sessions,
and seven books there on the shelf, no more.

gush

gush remorse, and gush the hurt out
gush the fury, gush the anger
scream at life, get all the dirt out
wash your goddess clean, then thank her.

brief history of the world

God thought
"what shall i do today?
i'm bored. if there were sky
it would be grey

i know
i'll plant a wonder seed
evolving world!
give everyone all they need"

and this he did
over several nights
a magic kingdom!
just one thing
there was no light
(this was put right).

and then he gave us all free will
having lit up the place and more
and what do we do to thank him for this?
get greedy, fuck it all up, make war

and now it's a lamentable state
gift horse, mouth... comes to my mind
but He is ever loving, willing
"children, seek and ye shall find..."

i wonder if the Holy Mary ever had toothache

ave Maria piena di grazia
il Signore con te
searing fire inside my gum
right up to my nose
my gerbil face
my claret punishment, i see
my deal this month. ok.

tu sei benedetta fra le donne
and your arms full of roses
small kids hats like tea cosies
as you held the little Lord of all
who takest away the sins of the world
God, just take my tooth decay

e Benedetto è il frutto del tuo seno
and blessed are those who understand pain
for they benefit more from the joy, ecco-mi!
of prayer in these times
and solace, the comfort,
and all the love...
oh, all the love.
that's in my mouth.
Mary hold me tight tonight
now and in the hour of
my death
i'm not sure i can stand it
i'm rocking to help the
no way out
of the nails thru my feet
and pins thru my teeth.

ave Maria, madre di Dio
and mother of all daughters,
all mothers, all women
and all human beings
and make this hot poker
stop pushing up higher
up until
my cheekbones scream

you bled for us, you didn't complain
your tears are mixed in with this pus
oozing onto my tongue
your bleeding swirling
with the blood on my gums
your pain is my pain
Mary you are blessed indeed
all of the world is in your heart
and your arms full of ivy too

prega per noi peccatori
i understand that i am a sinner
oh yes, and a good'un too
i was often a monster to mum
in illness and deep despair
oh yes, to the one most sacred to me
an angel, indeed.
how dare i, a pip?
a nothing, a spec
upset my Mary,
my only mother, my cord?

adesso e nell'ora della nostra morte
and when i die i will fall into His arms
your arms will be carrying him as your own
your arms i am in
and Ave Maria,
i pray to you now
as the throbbing continues
i look like a wilson
and still lack the confidence
this type of raft
but suffer it i do
and shall till it's dead

Holy Mother, pray for me now
and the fire inside my face today
the red, red heart
pulsating in anger
at what i've become
i could've been better
and served you more hours
and thought more of others

and taken their pain
and comforted them
while i waited in line at the grotty stage door
stuck, and still stuck in my taps on the floor

Ave Maria
queen of heaven
if this is just tooth ache
i'll have it each day
to show you my reverence
give it to me!
give me more pain
and i'll suffer it for you
i think i can feel you,
some days, very strongly
and i so want one
but if i cannot have one
i feel that's because
i am yet
your newborn
i don't mean Jesus
i mean your poor daughter
i'll take what i'm given
and carry my cross
to the doctor, the dentist
your blooms in my heart
you are the woman
the one woman only
who feels like another
cord-mother to me

ave Maria, piena di grazia
if you never had tooth ache
i'll have it for you.

leaving blue

i wanted to talk, but how could i?
feared it might mean less than nothing to you
if i told you the truth about me
and the last few years
what with pain and with death
i've been blue, but deep blue, not the sea

but now i am healthy
my sun she is wealthy
and hope has arrived
wings glowing with pride

i think that you've been badly burned
all my letters, all returned
and dear,
now you're bleaker
and darker and weaker
than ever i knew
could be drawn in
to you.

it's also ironic
that one love platonic
could make me seek solace
from thoughts of a get out.
yes, i am still here.
but are you still out there?

i wanted to talk, but how could i?
•

for lucy

skidding down a mole hole slide
to human eye, hilarious
with brandenburgs and cake for tea
and chit chat, quite gregarious
they spoke of most important stuff
like bubbles, mermaids, circles, fairs
i was encouraged to take part
(thank God it wasn't current affairs).

boys they will be boys, for sure,
i hope it gives them pleasure
i'd rather deal in even less inches
alice, tea, and dance a measure

our tilly mint

there once was a soft girl called tilly
as ambitious as she was silly
this hair-brained young bint
went from broke, being skint
to matching the mint of prince willy

rain again

oh, but i love it!

the sheer relief of not going out in it,
but
hiding, blind-folded
walk round naked
just floating around
and opening red wine
and generally being a
kimono clad wafty thing
a scented lithe being
with my hands down my
yoga pants for some release
and locked-in and dreaming
in carb driven heaven
smiling in comfort
of hard rain again

thinking of how i am lucky to have him
knowing i'm blessed
when others keep breaking up
we stay together.
in poverty i found
my soul billionaire!
millions of kisses and doing my hair
protecting and stroking
and making me weep
holding me all thru the night
when we sleep.
trillions of thoughts about chopin, debussy
ravel and my lindsay dan, nyro, and bowie
all of the loving and
all the forgiving
and nothing compares to his complex character.
with those looks could be a model or actor
but it's in these moments that i smile the most
at nothing
we've nothing!

it's chilly and pissing down
thinking bout constancy
what it has done for me
magicked the pain away
and it's another day

yes, and it's raining
it's sweet rain
again

post storm

i crossed five fields just after the storm
it stayed grey, ghostly, misty dawn
slipped in the mud, a fall never matters
i was so happy, i'd mend all the tatters
and wash off the blood and have my wrist fixed
for when you have faith, you are safe in the styx.

my life hangs on your words

my life hangs on your words
my life hangs on your words

not because i'm sad
or because i'm slightly mad
eros came thru my willow tree
and pointed at me

you're in love

deeply deeply deeply...
so pity me, in ecstasy
needy needy needy...
one more sorry little junkie
lost at sea

my life hangs on your words
my life hangs on your words

icing or death

you go into the affair
like a martian falling from the sky
and you've no idea why,
no, you just don't know why

like a hole in your boat
you watch your house fill up
you float for a bit
and feel closer to heaven
then you watch yourself drown
you go down
you go down

oh, love, sweet bitter love
why must you hurt us?
i cannot see why
we ever should suffer

but how we adore
the beginning, the joy
when we're playing our soul
for a dangerous toy

the act of love is as icing to cake
there cannot be any small falsehood or fakeness
and those that hear no music
then hear the endless symphony!
and those that see only darkness
so, they eat the rainbow, when
there is a choice: icing or death
to love or to die

the human's urge, i think,
has always been to fly.

that irresistible
wanting to be one
the ache of the moon
and the pull of the sun

the longing's the best bit.
all stopped in perfection
stuck in that bliss
with everything lit
from candles to senses
can't ever seal love, though
for it's perfection
and thus it will go

we were on fire
and it all came to pass
our need was so urgent
we lost it so fast

white dreams on a black charger

i have never had a nightmare
and i think that's most unusual
i only dream of daily practices
like washing up

and then recurred a million times
on dreaded stamp perusal
and packing up my school bag
and making bread
or tidying up

i never dream in colour
yet my art is full to busting:
orange, amber,
perugino blue
and gold encrusting.
every thwacking hue!

i do not dream of romance
though my mind is full of it
and sometimes when i dream
it's plain, mundane, and
worse, it has no wit

i never catch myself at sleep
afloat above a roof top
and yet all thru my waking life
fey flights of fancy spin non-stop

i do the sort of stuff that bores
the daily grind, the drag
like stopping at the printer's store or
looking thru my bag

it sort of comes out in reverse
night terrors pass me by
white dreams on a black charger
i suppose...

i don't know why.

if you could have seen them

if you could have seen them speed
and rush to grab the 'next big thing'
you'd smirk with me, and laugh with one
who crawls around a canvas on her knees
and has fifty pence tucked into her sweat pants
and hung up the laces of being hung up
and hid her spinning wheel, all spun out
tired of all the twats

if you could have seen them push
each other over in the mud
for fame and fools celebrity
that makes you rich with travesty
gross lack of authenticity
i don't get it
i can't see
and thus it quite escapes me

what i want is a piano here
a pencil there
and be near to the sea
a book just for my poetry
and a voice to sing it out freely
and the longest expression
of fire in my soul,
once caged
but now set free.
yes! *i'm finally free*!

if you could have seen them
chasing tenners, you would snigger too
so come, take my hand
and we will wander
thru the lion's den
watching art get murdered again and again
and poor and mocked, we're thrift shop dressed
screaming, laughing, but fulfilled, yes

thank me and go

i gave all my cash to a one legged tramp
it lit up my grace like a tiffany lamp
and if i were half of God's plan i know i should
give all of my jewels and my bag. i just stood
there, naked in public, and cold in this charity
shock, authenticity, there's a community
innocent love had swelled up in me so
one tear, he said "thank you" and then watched me go.

journey

i walked along the track bare feet
the wind swept sand right down my throat
i kept on the path and kept reading north
the journey you sing on one note

i thought about what could have been
the wind swept sand in my eyes
my pace became more and more marked in time
the journey where everyone dies

pin

i see a pin
and shrivel up in
instant atrophy

i know it will
and when it pricks
the will within me,
yes, will strive
to survive, oh, me!
oh God! and wilful ever!
"vanish to the hills, please go"
to my other self,
and you stay far,
and far away
a breath away
from everybody else
you see?

it will feel just like a chain saw
touching bone
and all my frame
and worse, my mind
slices into old wounds now
re-open them for me to grieve.
thought that i was over that bridge...

pain calls here:
"you'll come to me
and beautifully soon
i've got you still,
and i've always owned you
fragile little girl
you'll fight till
you beg for it, suffer so, you'll swoon"
again and again
it wants me to fail
and crumble under the mountain's weight
and others cannot even tell
i'm scared
i play the game well...

that pin is glaring straight at me
to pick it up and stab myself
right thru my upper lip, i know,
i see thru clear glass, both sides how
when i am in it, deep just now
and tiny nothings have me floored
and broken into tiny pieces
never to be fixed again,

"this one's best left, walk on here."
my instinct always knows the score.

the pin's still on the floor.

treasure

we all know this guy takes his pleasure
from cucbicles, coke, wit and young men at leisure
and pompusly jokes
with no hint of reproach
in fact he's a national trasure

the soul, the sea

this is where i want to land
not for sorrow, not for sand
i heard you calling silk, slash sea
and silver, whooshing surf on me

luscious, circle, oozing bubble,
glamour gowns in satin, rubble,
rocks that hurt and heal together
lost a seagull, found a feather

this is mine, the promised place
tread on broken glass, blood's face,
the joy of full immersion's band
you'll hear it while you die on land

don't feel pretty here, or care
i want grit stuck in my hair
i want oil stains and the pleasure
trance and drink an ocean measure!

and for treasure, water's space
so vast here is the merman's grace
that overwhelms me and i claw
his back, his power feeds me more

and rolling over driftwood, chasing
sun and sky and more embracing
i don't sing, i'm mute at sea.

i just hear what it sings to me.

advice from insensitives

the stupidest coupling of words seems to me
to be those from a friend, ruling off with 'be happy'

as if you could be, you're choosing your pain
and having been down, want to go there again

it's dense, doesn't help, if well meaning, and surely
it can't be thought out, can it, unless *they're* poorly?

don't tell me they've chosen and hand picked that phrase,
not computing contentment is all that we crave

or at least a reprieve from this endless black dog
returning, tail wagging, our friend from the fog.

it's up there with 'be well', the do-gooders faux-pas
as if it's your choice to *get aids* or go ga-ga

the best they come up with is crass as it's rude,
an order, to boot, like "i told you, be good!"

"just pull yourself up by your boot strings, don't stress"
insensitives, in themselves, oh! uber blessed

the lot of them, morons, i think you'll agree
well wishes from 'a' can be last straws for 'b'.

hans

the once was a brilliant pianist, hans
but a terrible crash lost him both of his hands
he turned it to humour,
a show with jokes in it
the people all loved him,
and fame came in minutes.

if you're on a mission
go forth with suspicion...
you want to make God laugh?
just tell Him your plans!

breathe in, fall, rise, go

like a whirling top possessed...
go round girl, go round!
and let your hair shoot out and fly after you
catapult springing and spiriting water
catching you up every time, but not quite
letting the sweat fly and shoot off your face
twirl faster and faster
and manifest laughter
your movement, sonorous
bright thru the air

she moves as she's singing
yes! a green garden spring
massaging wet in the desperate grass
go for your life, lover
twist round in your fire
see things in purple
and get called a liar
for you it's tuned to nothing
just air from the higher ground
when you get dizzy
go faster. eat danger.
laugh at it all
you lose your next layer
with motion, not painful
hot hips lead the way
tripping on no-knees
your feet are hot hopping
on white coals and dropping
out everything that goes against
your one sweet cause

it's been too long, little one
since you've let go, and you
don't have to please anyone
it's your game!
and you're in your sphere here
getting it better
the roundling of life
is the the circle of sex
so dance till your flames
are the whitest and best

dance till you fly,
if you slow down
you're punished
you'll burn out,
you're hexed
if you doubt it
you're next

my panther

he looks just like a sleeping panther
dark and smooth and calm
and when there was the earthquake
he pounced wild to shield me from harm

his air's just like a baby.
scent-sweet first in their secret breaths
he is my soul, and i am so proud
not to have settled for less.

he prowls around bologna
a strange figure, inkily clad
he gives me all his honesty
which makes me happy, sometimes sad

he lies on his right side, and
i like to lie on my left
his eyes are always open
if i wake at night, bereft

his prancing, though, it runs straight thru me
he roars thru my heart
i've watched this cat for years now
i feel it's just the start

yes, i'm living with a wild thing
his elegance and flair
we think we live in a luxury flat
it's really a primitive lair

he's made of utmost beauty too
all dark and subdued, blacks,
let it be known that big cats all
adore it when you scratch their backs

and when we're under the sleepy tree
and front to front we're lying
sometimes he sets about my flesh
and pleasure mounts until i'm crying

sleep sleep

sleep, sleep come to me
brush my forehead with your wing
hint to me you're on your way, oh!
just one muddled thought, i'll know,
then i regain my faith, and mend,
forego incarceration's end

sleep, sleep, make fall my fears
kiss my eyelids with your tears
when i weep it's for the day
i need your light, i weep and pray
so feed my lows and hurt my bones
and i'm in shackles, stuck with woes

sleep, sleep come to me
end this night-shift agony
i'll love you soon as i am able
tortured girls become unstable
sick, but when you seek me out
i'll softly cling, within without

i see what i see

"you would see the dust falling down form the sky..."
he told me in '93

"and you'll see so much more that you don't want to see"

a old man wanking in his car at sarzana
he said
"if you look for it,
then you will see.
only you'd look for that type of thing
and only you would see it"
i told him, sincerely,
"i see what i see."

but his sentence slashed my ears forever
perverted my clean queen, one more trojan whore,
i feel what i fear, it's as common as jeans
and when i get just that bit sorted, i'm near

i see what i see,
and i show what feels true to me
you're unaware that
i'm sorting it all out
i'm facing my rampant dogs
and that empowers me
a good job is done
but it's done rather painfully.

when people start with "you know what your problem is"
i always say "oh, only too well, but, see
i also see yours is massive, and frankly
i think i got off, by comparison, lightly"

thing is,
i just see what i see.

conversation

"when you look at your creations
all that love surrounding you...
no-one ever could feel sorrow"
so i say "i do"

i am a lab. rat

the drugs they all poured into me
are coming out duly and finally
they couldn't shut me up, you see
the pain was not imaginary
conditions come, diseases go
but mine it stayed thru sun and snow
for twenty eight full quadrants turning
all the sweating, screaming, burning

sun! the torture hit a halt
but now i was a chemical vault
up to them to write the script
up to me, to quit the shit
drawing hour by hour for years
starts and middles, vomit, tears
but ends in sensitivity
and seeing like i'd never seen
and loving like i'd always loved
so give a nod to Him above
for many still are stuck in hell
livers stiff with shock as well

(in iatrogenic struggle
little attention, little desire
i suffered more
on the medical scrap heap
thirty years of knife-life headaches
sickness, anaemia, stuttering, shakes
falling over, and fainting and blackouts
and crying to see others do what i do
on top of what i had been cursed with already
just from meds they had over prescribed
the whole thing became convoluted, contrived
to make them feel useful
they hadn't a clue
the caring profession!
no work and no interest
i won't forget
that they cared even less).

the gush of life poetry
paintings flood out of me
music set free, and melting onto the keys
and singing, dancing, yes! yes! all of these
are back from the slammer and into the flesh.
and seeing life all new and white linen fresh

(and now i know
it was due to those fuckers,
in gestadt every time
that you need them
– did you know ninety percent of those demi-gods
finished up bottom of their sorry class? –
those are the ones
who have got your mum's life line
sat right in the palm of their
arrogant hands.
insured to the hilt
not so squeaky clean,
drug dealers, quacks
fob you off, and get worshipped...)

now i can't stand to waste even a minute
from now on, no, not with one dark dot inside it
all i want is to be back on stage
to give of my heart, my time, and my age
my comfort, my wisdom to others in hell
still fighting the damned, we keep fighting as well...
never give up! "it's hopeless, i've tried"

it all comes out, hear me, what's trapped deep inside.

misunderstood

the stars all bemoan that they're misunderstood
and that's why it sounds like a whinge when they sing
well...
the most misunderstood person i've met is me
and i couldn't care less, 'cause i think it's a good thing!

threatened trust

the lyrics in me bend the bowers,
as we caress the wilder flowers
the cynic in me mocks this spirit
and the trusting that goes with it

noli me tollere

that church at sorso
sees me
still sat
in all
my humility
the monks are
brown and bearded
they're called
the cappuccini

the first time that i visited
was in a fearful storm,
but as we entered, down rocks fell
i was staggered, choked, unwell

the love light in that little space
cannot be told
you must go there!
you must see
yes, you will see
that all that glisters is not gold

Maria reigns her glory blue
and such celeste intense
and all you see is clouded
in His pain for her
and faint with incense

i kneel for her
i bow for her
i see my prayers inside my head
i picture loved ones, happy, safe
i want to suffer in their stead

and i am going there just now
and i will sit and weep for her
and it will flood me with soul ease
i need it more than ever.

bet

an a.s.b.o. took a bet
"nick everything that you can get"
so he stole a cat
and he loved it so much that
he's now a respectable vet

scent

taking me back
to where i was last time
i caught it
this power
so woozy, particular
myriad, mountain
of pointillist dots
still one discovers new
ones, yes, and hourly

this one, white sheets
on the south coast of england
sickness, and writhing in
great pain, and that gift
the perfume
to cheer me.
so kind the thought.
smell it now
i get sick
violence strikes up
inside of me, there

that one, in amber
the touch of a rug
making love in the autumn
the glow on his face
the tongue, and the firelighters
auburn dog flopping
and lovers rolling in joy

the other side, calm rain
fresh fall in april
the out and out heaven of feeling alive
alone, loved and whole
violet the colour... seep thru my shirt
and be see thru
give joy!

when i smell april rain today
i glow from my solar plexus
right thru my soul
radiate my content
this monumental ecstasy
in which we were...
well i was.
(you left me
for a boy)

yes, because it rained that day
it was easier to go.

girl in red

"girl in red,
honey, i don't see how you can say
you're ready for his beddy yet"

teddy says
"oh baby, squeeze me harder and faster"
five little hairs upon his chest

she's little miss hips and tits now
i don't know where she got it but
she's got it going on,
and how

she says
"my taxi will be coming
gotta shower!
i gotta get it on and off
within an hour
mummy,
i'm not blanking what you said, but
this girl's staying in red.
yes!
this girl's staying in red".

no justice at all

i saw a bouncing large mosquito
though i often see whats not
he was over our kitchen hob, yes
i was in situ, ready to swat

i lived that moment spiritually
"i'll let him be, i'll set him free"
and what was my reward for this?
that night he dot to dotted me.

the sin of the siren

what did she do to be labelled so harshly
and such a thing despised
she sang so beautifully, such power
that all men were terrified.

they'd follow her sounds wherever they led
the magnet pulled so fast
she was the way and they couldn't resist
they left it all, wet in the past

and went from level and into height
and felt that throbbing beat
her singing lured them, one by one
pushed on by their fate, not their feet

she was the guilt for which they longed
she was the other world
she was desire, their wings all tight
until with raw lust they unfurled

the sailors, mesmerized, chased up that voice
and left their ships all sunk
she was the red cup of blood and of desire
that had them hard and drunk

this was the sin of the siren
her sexuality:
and given this role, she would play it and use it

but she's no worse than me

index of titles